## **Tablet Of Content**

Disclaimer .................................................................3
Introduction ..............................................................5
What is a stock market? ...........................................7
Summary of the Jamaican stock market....................8
What affects a market ..............................................9
Different types of investing .....................................12
Steps to invest in the Jamaican stock market..........15
What is bond investing? .........................................19
Mutual Fund Investing............................................21
What is stock investing? .........................................23
Brokers in Jamaica .................................................26
Terms to know .......................................................27
Case study - Covid19..............................................34
Conclusion .............................................................35

# Author
## Javone Mitchell

# **Disclaimer**

The information provided in this book, "Investing in Jamaica's Stock Market," is for educational and informational purposes only. While every effort has been made to ensure the accuracy and reliability of the content, the author and publisher make no representations or warranties, express or implied, regarding the completeness, suitability, or validity of the information presented. Investing in the stock market involves inherent risks, including the risk of loss of capital. The content of this book does not constitute financial advice, and readers are encouraged to conduct their own research and consult with a qualified financial advisor before making any investment decisions.

The author and publisher disclaim any liability for any direct, indirect, incidental, special, or consequential damages arising out of or in any way connected with the use or reliance on the information provided in this book. Readers are solely responsible for their investment decisions and actions taken based on the information contained herein.

Furthermore, the performance of investments in Jamaica's stock market may be subject to various economic, political, and regulatory factors, which can impact investment outcomes. Past performance is not indicative of future results, and no guarantee or assurance can be given that any particular investment strategy or approach will be successful.

Readers should also be aware that the stock market can be volatile, and prices of securities can fluctuate widely in response to market conditions and other factors. It is important to exercise caution and prudence when investing in the stock market and to consider one's own risk tolerance and investment objectives before entering the market.

By reading this book, readers acknowledge and accept the risks associated with investing in Jamaica's stock market and agree to hold harmless the author and publisher from any claims, losses, or damages that may arise from their use of the information provided herein.

# Introduction

Welcome to the exciting world of investing in the Jamaican Stock Exchange (JSE), where opportunities abound for those ready to embark on their journey towards financial growth and prosperity. In recent years, the Jamaican stock market has emerged as a dynamic and thriving arena, attracting both local and international investors seeking avenues for wealth creation and portfolio diversification.

In this book, "Investing in the Jamaican Stock Exchange" we embark on a comprehensive exploration of the JSE, providing beginners with the essential knowledge, tools, and strategies needed to navigate this market with confidence and success.

As we journey together through the pages of this book, you will discover the rich tapestry of opportunities that the Jamaican stock market offers, from blue-chip companies to emerging sectors poised for growth. You will learn how to evaluate stocks, assess risk, and construct a diversified portfolio tailored to your investment objectives and risk tolerance.

Whether you aspire to build long-term wealth, save for retirement, or achieve financial independence, investing in the Jamaican Stock Exchange offers a myriad of opportunities for investors of all backgrounds and experience levels. With the right knowledge, mindset, and guidance, you can unlock the full potential of the JSE and embark on a rewarding journey towards financial success.

So, join me as we embark on this enlightening journey into the world of investing in the Jamaican Stock Exchange. Let this book be your road map to prosperity and financial empowerment in the vibrant landscape of the Jamaican stock market.

# What is a stock market?

A stock market is a platform or exchange where buyers and sellers trade shares of publicly listed companies. It provides a marketplace for investors to buy and sell ownership stakes in companies, which are represented by stocks or shares. The stock market plays a crucial role in capital formation for companies and provides investors with opportunities to participate in the financial success of these companies. Prices of stocks are determined by market forces of supply and demand, and stock markets serve as a key indicator of economic health and investor sentiment.

## Summary of the Jamaican stock market

The Jamaican stock market, officially known as the Jamaica Stock Exchange (JSE), is a dynamic financial marketplace facilitating the buying and selling of securities. Established in 1969, the JSE has evolved into a key player in the Caribbean region. It lists a variety of securities, including stocks, bonds, and mutual funds. The market's performance is influenced by factors such as economic trends, regulatory developments, and global influences. Investors engaging in the Jamaican stock market encounter opportunities in sectors like tourism, agriculture, and technology. The regulatory environment shapes investor activities, and strategies must consider the unique risks associated with this developing market. Overall, the Jamaican stock market provides a platform for capital formation, investment growth, and economic development in the region.

# What affects a market

- **Indicators:** Economic data such as GDP growth, unemployment rates, inflation, and consumer confidence can significantly influence investor sentiment and market trends.

- **Interest Rates:** Central bank decisions on interest rates can affect borrowing costs for businesses and consumers, influencing spending and investment decisions.

- **Corporate Earnings:** The financial performance of individual companies, as reflected in their earnings reports, can drive stock prices. Positive earnings often lead to higher stock valuations.

- **Global Events:** International developments, geopolitical events, and global economic trends can impact markets worldwide, affecting the stock prices of multinational companies.

- **Market Sentiment:** Investor perception and confidence play a crucial role. Positive news and optimism can drive buying activity, while negative sentiment can lead to selling.

- **Government Policies:** Fiscal and monetary policies, as well as regulatory changes, can impact businesses and industries, affecting their stock prices.

- **Technological Advances:** Innovations and advancements in technology can influence stock prices, especially for companies in the technology sector.

- **Natural Disasters and Pandemics:** Unforeseen events such as natural disasters or health crises, like the COVID-19 pandemic, can have profound effects on economic activities and stock markets.

- **Currency Fluctuations:** Changes in currency values can impact companies that operate internationally, affecting their revenue and profit margins.

- **Commodity Prices:** For countries heavily reliant on commodities, fluctuations in prices of commodities like oil, gold, or agricultural products can impact their stock markets.

- **Market Speculation:** Investor behavior and speculative trading can contribute to short-term fluctuations in stock prices.

# Different types of investing

- **Value Investing:** Focuses on identifying undervalued stocks trading below their intrinsic value. Investors believe these stocks have potential for future growth, providing an opportunity for long-term gains.

- **Growth Investing:** Seeks stocks with strong potential for above-average growth in earnings and revenue. Investors are willing to pay a premium for these stocks in anticipation of future appreciation.

- **Dividend Investing:** Prioritizes stocks that consistently pay dividends. Suited for income-focused investors looking for regular cash flow along with the potential for capital appreciation.

- **Income Investing:** Targets assets that generate a steady stream of income, not limited to dividends (e.g., bonds, real estate investment trusts - REITs).

Prioritizes regular income over significant capital gains.

- **Momentum Investing:** Capitalizes on the momentum of stocks that have recently performed well. Assumes that stocks that have been rising will continue to do so in the short term.

- **Day Trading:** Intraday buying and selling of stocks within the same trading day. Requires close monitoring of market movements and technical analysis.

- **Swing Trading:** Capitalizes on short to medium-term price movements. Traders aim to capture "swings" in the market, holding positions for several days to weeks.

- **Buy and Hold:** Long-term investment strategy where investors buy stocks and hold onto them for an extended period. Based on the belief that, over time, the market tends to grow, and short-term fluctuations are less relevant.

- **Sector Rotation:** Investors shift their investments among different sectors based on economic or market trends. Aims to capitalize on the cyclical nature of various industries.

- **Quality Investing:** Focuses on high-quality stocks with strong fundamentals, such as consistent earnings growth and low debt. Aims for stability and long-term appreciation.

Investors often tailor these strategies to their risk tolerance, financial goals, and time horizons. Combining multiple strategies or adopting a hybrid approach is also common.

## Steps to invest in the Jamaican stock market

1. **Educate Yourself:**

• Learn the basics of stock market investing, understand financial terms, and familiarize yourself with the specific dynamics of the Jamaican stock market.

2. **Define Your Financial Goals and Risk Tolerance:**

• Clarify your investment objectives, whether they're focused on long-term growth, income, or a combination. Assess your risk tolerance to determine the level of risk you're comfortable with.

3. **Open a Brokerage Account:**

• Choose a reputable brokerage firm that facilitates trades on the Jamaican stock exchange. Ensure that the brokerage provides access to the Jamaican market and offers the services you need.

4. **Complete Necessary Documentation:**

• Fulfill the required documentation to open a brokerage account. This may include providing identification, proof of address, and other relevant information.

5. **Fund Your Account:**

• Deposit funds into your brokerage account. Ensure that you understand the deposit and withdrawal procedures of the chosen brokerage.

6. **Research Stocks:**

• Conduct thorough research on Jamaican stocks. Analyze financial statements, company performance, and industry trends. Stay updated on news and events that may impact the market.

7. **Diversify Your Portfolio:**

• Avoid putting all your funds into a single stock. Diversify your portfolio across different sectors and industries to spread risk.

8. **Place Your Trades:**

• Use the brokerage platform to place buy or sell orders for the selected stocks. Pay attention to market orders, limit orders, and other order types available on the platform.

9. **Monitor Your Investments:**

• Regularly check the performance of your investments. Stay informed about any news or events that might affect the stocks in your portfolio.

10. **Consider Professional Advice:**

• If you're unsure about investment decisions, seek advice from financial professionals or investment advisors familiar with the Jamaican market.

11. **Understand Fees and Charges:**

• Be aware of the fees and charges associated with buying and selling stocks, as well as any other fees your brokerage may impose.

12. **Stay Informed About Regulations:**

• Keep abreast of any regulatory changes or updates in the Jamaican stock market that may affect your investments.

Remember, investing always carries risks, and it's crucial to make decisions based on careful consideration and research. If you're new to investing, consider consulting with a financial advisor to help you navigate the complexities of the market and tailor your strategy to your financial goals.

# What is bond investing?

Bond investing involves purchasing debt securities issued by governments, municipalities, corporations, or other entities. When you invest in bonds, you are essentially lending money to the bond issuer in exchange for periodic interest payments and the return of the principal amount at maturity.

**Here are the key components of bond investing:**

A bond is a fixed-income instrument that represents a loan made by an investor to a borrower (the issuer). Bonds have a face value, also known as the principal or par value, which is the amount the issuer promises to repay at maturity. Bonds pay periodic interest to bondholders. The interest rate is determined at the time of issuance and is known as the coupon rate. Interest payments are typically made semi-annually, annually, or according to the terms specified in the bond's indenture. Bonds also have a specified maturity date when the issuer repays the principal to the bondholders. Investors can choose from bonds with varying maturities, ranging from short-term (less than one year) to long-term ( usually a couple years). The market value of existing bonds can fluctuate based on changes in interest rates, credit quality, and other market conditions.

**Types of Bonds:**

- Government Bonds: Issued by national governments.

- Corporate Bonds: Issued by companies.

Bond investing can provide a steady stream of income, capital preservation, and diversification benefits. However, it's important to carefully assess the risk and return profile of different bonds and consider factors such as interest rate movements, economic conditions, and the creditworthiness of issuers.

# Mutual Fund Investing

A mutual fund is a pooled investment vehicle that gathers money from many investors and uses that money to buy a diversified portfolio of stocks, bonds, or other securities. Each investor in the mutual fund owns shares, which represent a portion of the holdings of the fund.

**Here are key aspects of mutual fund investing:**

Mutual funds are managed by professional fund managers or management teams who make investment decisions on behalf of the investors. Mutual funds offer diversification by investing in a variety of assets. This helps spread risk and reduces the impact of poor performance from any individual security. There are various types of mutual funds catering to different investment objectives. Common categories include equity funds, bond funds, money market funds, and balanced funds. The value of one share in a mutual fund is known as the

Net Asset Value (NAV). It represents the fund's total assets minus its total liabilities. Mutual funds are generally liquid, allowing investors to buy or sell shares on any business day at the fund's closing NAV. Profits earned from the fund's investments are distributed to investors in the form of dividends or capital gains. Investors can choose to reinvest these distributions or receive them as cash. Different mutual funds have different risk profiles based on their underlying investments. Investors should match the risk level of a fund with their own risk tolerance and investment goals. Some mutual funds have minimum investment requirements, while others may have no minimums.

Mutual funds provide an accessible way for investors to participate in the financial markets without directly managing a portfolio of individual securities. Investors can choose funds based on their financial goals, risk tolerance, and investment preferences.

# What is stock investing?

Stock investing involves buying shares or ownership stakes in publicly traded companies with the expectation that the value of those shares will increase over time. Investors who engage in stock investing are referred to as stockholders or shareholders. Stocks are also known as equities or securities.

**Here are key elements of stock investing:**

When you buy shares of a company's stock, you become a partial owner of that company. The number of shares you own determines your ownership percentage. Stock investors aim to profit from capital appreciation, which occurs when the market value of their shares increases over the purchase price. Some companies distribute a portion of their profits to shareholders in the form of dividends. Dividend stocks can provide a steady income stream in addition to the potential for capital gains. Stock prices are influenced by various factors, including the company's financial performance, market conditions, economic trends, and investor sentiment. As a result, stock values can fluctuate over time. Investors may adopt long-term or short-term strategies. Long-term investors typically buy and hold stocks for an extended period, while short-term investors (traders) may buy and sell stocks quickly to capitalize on short-term price movements. Successful stock investing often involves thorough research and analysis. Investors examine a company's financial statements, earnings reports, industry trends, and other relevant information to make informed decisions. Diversification involves spreading investments across different stocks and sectors to reduce risk. A well-diversified portfolio can help protect against poor performance in any single stock or industry. Stock investing comes with risks, including the potential for loss of capital. Investors need to assess their risk tolerance and choose stocks that align with their investment goals and comfort level with risk. Investors typically need a brokerage account to buy and sell stocks. Online brokerages make it convenient for individuals to trade stocks through user-friendly platforms. Stocks are bought and sold on stock exchanges, such as the Jamaican stock exchange. The exchange facilitates the trading of securities among buyers and sellers. Investors can place market orders, where they buy or sell at the current market price, or limit orders, where they set a specific price at which they are willing to buy or sell.

Stock investing provides individuals with the opportunity to participate in the growth and success of publicly traded companies. However, it's important to note that the stock market carries inherent risks, and prices can be volatile. Therefore, investors should carefully consider their financial goals and conduct thorough research before making investment decisions.

# Brokers in Jamaica

1. BARITA INVESTMENTS
2. JMMB INVESTMENTS
3. NCB CAPITAL MARKET
4. JN FUND MANAGER
5. MAYBERRY INVESTMENTS
6. SAGICOR INVESTMENTS
7. VM WEALTH MANAGER
8. PROVEN WEALTH LIMITED

### Requirements
- ID
- Proof of Address
- Proof of Income
- TRN
- 2 Reference
- Funding ( **as low as $1000 jmd** )

Please note that this may vary based on your broker. Contact your preferred broker to confirm.

## Terms to know

Understanding key terms related to the Jamaican Stock Exchange (JSE) can enhance your knowledge of stock market operations. Here are some terms to know:

• **Jamaica Stock Exchange (JSE):** The primary stock exchange in Jamaica where securities such as stocks and bonds are bought and sold.

• **Listed Company:** A company whose shares are officially traded on the JSE.

• **Stock Broker:** A licensed professional or firm that facilitates the buying and selling of stocks on behalf of investors.

• **Stock Market Index:** A measure of the performance of a group of stocks representing a particular market segment. In Jamaica, common indices include the JSE Main Index and the JSE Combined Index.

• **Market Capitalization:** The total value of a company's outstanding shares of stock, calculated by multiplying the current stock price by the number of shares.

• **Dividend:** A portion of a company's profits distributed to its shareholders. Dividends can be paid in cash or additional shares.

• **Bull Market:** A market characterized by rising stock prices, investor optimism, and a positive economic outlook.

• **Bear Market:** A market characterized by falling stock prices, investor pessimism, and a negative economic outlook.

• **Initial Public Offering (IPO):** The first time a company's stock becomes available for public purchase on the stock exchange.

• **Additional public offering (APO):** The company is offering additional shares to the market after the stocks has been listed to the stock exchange.

• **Securities:** Financial instruments traded on the stock market, including stocks, bonds, and other investment products.

- **Blue-Chip Stocks:** Shares of well-established, financially stable, and reputable companies with a history of reliable performance.

- **Brokerage Fee:** The fee charged by a stockbroker for executing buy or sell orders on behalf of an investor.

- **Market Order:** An order to buy or sell a security at the current market price.

- **Limit Order:** An order to buy or sell a security at a specific price or better.

- **Bid Price:** The highest price a buyer is willing to pay for a security.

- **Ask Price:** The lowest price a seller is willing to accept for a security.

- **Earnings per Share (EPS):** A company's profit divided by its number of outstanding shares. It indicates a company's profitability on a per-share basis.

- **Book Value:** The net asset value of a company, calculated by subtracting liabilities from assets.

- **Bourse:** An alternative term for a stock exchange; in Jamaica, it's commonly used interchangeably with the term "stock exchange."

- **Market Maker:** A firm or individual that facilitates the buying and selling of securities by providing liquidity in the market.

- **Halted:** A stock halt, or trading halt, is a temporary suspension of trading on a particular stock by the stock exchange. It can occur for various reasons such as pending news announcements, significant price movements, regulatory concerns, or market volatility. During a halt, investors cannot buy or sell shares of the halted stock until trading resumes. Halt duration vary depending on the reason and exchange regulations, ranging from minutes to days.

- **Portfolio:** A collection of financial investments (stocks, bonds, etc.) held by an individual or institution.

- **Volatility:** The degree of variation of a trading price series over time. High volatility indicates significant price fluctuations.

- **Broker:** A person or firm that facilitates the buying and selling of financial securities on behalf of clients.

- **ROI (Return on Investment):** A measure of the profitability of an investment, expressed as a percentage of the initial investment.

- **Stock Split:** An action where a company divides its existing shares into multiple shares, often to make them more affordable for investors.

- **Day Trading:** Buying and selling financial instruments within the same trading day to take advantage of short-term price movements.

- **Market Watch:** Keeping track of the performance of selected stocks or the overall market.

- **Diversification:** Spreading investments across various assets to reduce risk.

- **Bonds:** Debt securities that represent a loan made by an investor to a borrower (usually a government or corporation).

- **Earnings Per Share (EPS):** A company's profit divided by its number of outstanding shares, indicating its profitability on a per-share basis.

- **P/E Ratio (Price-to-Earnings Ratio):** A valuation ratio calculated by dividing the market price per share by the earnings per share, providing insight into the market's expectations for a company's future earnings growth.

- **Asset Allocation:** The distribution of investments among different asset classes (e.g., stocks, bonds, cash) to achieve a desired balance of risk and return.

- **Liquidity:** The ease with which an asset can be bought or sold in the market without affecting its price.

- **Blue Chip Stocks:** Stocks of large, well-established, and financially sound companies with a history of stable performance.

- **NAV (Net asset value):** Net Asset Value (NAV) is a measure used in investment. It represents the per-share value of a fund's assets minus its liabilities.

The calculation of NAV involves dividing the total value of the fund's assets (such as stocks, bonds, cash, etc.) minus any liabilities (such as expenses or debts) by the total number of shares outstanding. This calculation is typically performed at the end of each trading day.

Mathematically, NAV can be expressed as:

**Total Assets** ( Minus ) **Total Liabilities**
Divided by
**Total Number of Shares Outstanding**

Investors often use NAV as a reference point to gauge the value of their investment in the fund. It's important to note that NAV represents the intrinsic value of the fund's assets at a specific point in time and may fluctuate based on changes in the value of the underlying investments.

These terms should provide a foundation for understanding the Jamaican Stock Exchange and the broader concepts related to stock market investing. If you're new to investing, it's beneficial to further research and familiarize yourself with these terms to make informed investment decisions.

# Case study - Covid19

There are multiple aspects that can cause the stock market to make drastic changes for example COVID 19. COVID 19 brought serious economic challenges to the world including Jamaica. One of the aspects of Jamaica that was affected was their stock market.

Background: Before the pandemic, the Jamaican stock market had been exhibiting positive trends, with steady growth in various sectors. However, the arrival of COVID-19 triggered a rapid shift in market dynamics, leading to unprecedented volatility and uncertainty.

Immediate Impact: As COVID-19 spread globally, concerns over its economic implications grew. In Jamaica, the stock market experienced a sharp decline in early 2020 as investors grappled with the uncertainty surrounding the pandemic. Major industries, such as tourism and hospitality, were particularly hard-hit ( negatively ), reflecting in the performance of related stocks.

# Conclusion

This goes to show that the stock market is heavily influenced by various factors and once there there are changes, companies belonging to these sectors with be affect whether positively or negative and there related stocks will show theses changes also in the market.

# Author's Info

Scan the barcode below to view the book details on Amazon.com .

Scan the barcode below to view the seller's page on Amazon.com .

www.ingramcontent.com/pod-product-compliance
Lightning Source LLC
Chambersburg PA
CBHW070956220526
45471CB00007B/3054